The Hindenburg Disaster

Other titles in the *American Disasters* series:

The Hindenburg Disaster

Doomed Airship

Victoria Sherrow

Enslow Publishers, Inc.

40 Industrial Road	PO Box 38
Box 398	Aldershot
Berkeley Heights, NJ 07922	Hants GU12 6BP
USA	UK

http://www.enslow.com

Library of Congress Cataloging-in-Publication Data

Sherrow, Victoria.
    The Hindenburg disaster : doomed airship / Victoria Sherrow.
        p. cm. — (American disasters)
    Includes bibliographical references and index.
    ISBN 0-7660-1554-8
    1. Hindenburg (Airship)—Juvenile literature. 2. Aircraft accidents—New
Jersey—Juvenile literature. [1. Hindenburg (Airship) 2. Airships. 3. Aircraft
accidents.] I. Title. II. Series.
    TL659.H5 S54   2001
    363.12'465—dc21
                          2001000545

Printed in the United States of America

10 9 8 7 6 5 4 3 2 1

To Our Readers:
We have done our best to make sure all Internet addresses in this book were active and
appropriate when we went to press. However, the author and the publisher have no
control over and assume no liability for the material available on those Internet sites
or on other Web sites they may link to. Any comments or suggestions can be sent by
e-mail to comments@enslow.com or to the address on the back cover.

Contents

The *Hindenburg* floats peacefully over Manhattan on May 6, 1937. Just hours later, the ship would burst into flames as it attempted to land in Lakehurst, N.J.

CHAPTER 1

Thirty-Four Seconds of Terror

A large crowd gathered in Lakehurst, New Jersey, on May 6, 1937. They had come to watch the famous *Hindenburg* land. The *Hindenburg* was a type of balloon aircraft called a zeppelin. People all over the world had heard about this huge "flying hotel." It was the largest aircraft ever built. Soon these spectators would see it for themselves.

That evening, the mighty airship arrived. It seemed to float in midair. People stared, and reporters took notes. A Chicago radio newsman, Herbert Morrison, stood among the crowd. He said, "Here it comes, ladies and gentlemen, and what a sight it is, a thrilling one, just a marvelous sight."[1] Another reporter said it "looked like a silver whale."[2]

Traffic halted as the *Hindenburg* floated overhead. Eighteen-year-old Hepburn Walker was one of those who stopped his car to look at it. He remembered, "You could see the passengers waving, and the crewmen. You see a big thing like that and you think it's hardly believable it can be flying."[3]

The *Hindenburg* weighed 240 tons and measured 804 feet from end to end. That is nearly as long as three football fields. Zeppelins carried heavy loads of mail as well as people. The *Hindenburg* could hold more than a hundred tons. Yet it reached speeds of eighty-four miles an hour.

There was no faster, more pleasant way to cross the ocean in 1937. Airplanes did not yet take passengers on such long commercial flights. People had to go by zeppelin

*T*his sketch from an advertising brochure shows passengers on board the *Hindenburg* enjoying the view through the ship's glass observation windows.

or by ship. Zeppelin tickets cost more, but they were faster. The *Hindenburg* made the trip in two and a half days. That was twice as fast as a ship. People who got seasick also preferred zeppelins.

Besides, zeppelins were clean and comfortable. The rooms were nicely furnished and had running water. Passengers enjoyed attractive lounges and tasty meals.

The German airships also had good safety records. The company that owned the *Hindenburg* had another large passenger airship called the *Graf Zeppelin.* Together these two zeppelins had flown more than one million miles. More than eighteen thousand passengers had landed safely.

Now spectators watched as the *Hindenburg* drifted closer to the ground. Passengers smiled and waved from the large glass windows. Some people snapped pictures.

A ground crew stood on the field. They were ready to grab the landing lines from the airship. They would attach these lines to winches during the landing.

For a moment, the airship stood nearly still. The motors stopped running. Suddenly, flames shot up from the *Hindenburg.* The blaze spread rapidly. Pieces of the zeppelin's shell burned like paper and fell to the ground. The ship trembled and fell forward. New fires shot up everywhere the flames landed. People screamed.

The spectators' looks changed from delight to horror. A glorious sight had become a deadly nightmare. A ground crewman yelled, "Run for your lives!"[4]

*T*he burning shell of the *Hindenburg* plunges to the ground. The ship burned up in just thirty-four seconds.

Terrified people jumped or fell out of the burning airship. One man cried out in German, "It is the end!"[5]

The airship burned within thirty-four seconds. The fire took the lives of thirty-six people. Many others were burned and injured. That tragic day in 1937 also marked the end of zeppelin travel.

The disaster sparked many questions. Why had the *Hindenburg* caught fire? Was it an accident—or not?

CHAPTER 2

Lighter Than Air

In the 1890s, a German count tried to build a new kind of dirigible. A dirigible is a gas-filled balloon that can be steered. Count Ferdinand von Zeppelin had loved flying since 1863. He had taken a balloon ride while visiting the United States. The balloon rose seven hundred feet. Below him lay St. Paul, Minnesota, and the Mississippi River.

Von Zeppelin was then a young officer in the German army. He thought the military could use balloons. From the air, they could scout enemy territory and plan attacks. But balloons were hard to control. The winds changed their direction.

Hot-air balloons were not new. In 1785, a French balloonist crossed the English Channel. Another Frenchman flew a nonrigid airship over Paris in 1852. Different inventors tested new kinds of balloons and flying machines. Alberto Santos-Dumont of Brazil became famous for his flights. He made the first dirigible that

*C*ount Ferdinand von Zeppelin was inspired to build airships after riding in a balloon like those pictured above in 1863.

could be steered in normal weather. His airships were nonrigid.

Von Zeppelin built airships with rigid frames. They held gas that was lighter than air. People laughed at the "Crazy Count" and said his "flying machines" would never work. Von Zeppelin said, "If airships are possible at all, then mine are possible."[1]

In 1900, Von Zeppelin finished his first dirigible (*LZ 1*). He carried out several test flights that year. Curious people came to watch. Journalist Ernst Lehmann was among them. He said the airship looked "like a gigantic caterpillar slowly creeping forward."[2] Five people were on board during one of the test flights. They soared thirteen hundred feet into the air and traveled 3.75 miles.

Von Zeppelin worked to improve each new airship. In 1908, his fourth airship (*LZ 4*) flew for twelve hours. By then, the count was famous. He and his wife had been using their savings to fund his work. Now many Germans sent him money and encouraging letters. Von Zeppelin formed a company. It began earning money after the German military ordered some airships. They were called "zeppelins."

Soon zeppelins were carrying passengers, too. In 1911, the *LZ 10* made nearly one hundred short flights in Europe. During World War I, the German military used zeppelins to drop bombs on England and France.

People in other countries built airships, too. They were less reliable than the German models. Through the years, dozens of people died in crashes or explosions.

Count Von Zeppelin died in 1917. Dr. Hugo Eckener became the new head of the Zeppelin Company. It began making airships for longer flights. These zeppelins used strong new engines that weighed less than older engines.

The company launched the *Graf Zeppelin* in 1928. The next year, it flew around the world in twenty-one days. In 1930, the *Graf Zeppelin* carried scientists to the Arctic. They studied the weather and geography. By 1935, this airship was making routine trips between Germany and Brazil.

The Zeppelin Company made plans to launch an even bigger airship. They had started building it in 1931. Hard times hit Germany, however. The company ran out of money for the project. In 1933, Adolf Hitler and his Nazi party took over the German government. The Nazis thought zeppelins could boost their prestige. They supported the Zeppelin Company and paid for the new airship. It was finished in 1936 and was named *Hindenburg.*

Hugo Eckener disliked the Nazis. He often criticized them. But he could not stop them from using zeppelins for political reasons. Black Nazi swastikas were painted on the zeppelins' tail fins. Nazis sailed zeppelins over Germany and dropped Nazi booklets and small Nazi flags. The Nazis broadcast speeches from loudspeakers mounted on the *Hindenburg.* Berlin hosted the Summer Olympic

When Adolph Hitler rose to power in Germany, he supported the production of zeppelins. He believed the airships would increase the prestige of his Nazi Party.

games in 1936. The Nazis planned a spectacular show. They painted Olympic rings on the sides of the *Hindenburg.*

The *Hindenburg* was an awesome piece of work. It had a lightweight aluminum frame. Inside were sixteen huge cells (bags) filled with gas. Both the *Graf Zeppelin* and

Nazis painted swastikas on the *Hindenburg's* tail fins. They often used the airship to litter the ground from above with Nazi flags and booklets.

Hindenburg used hydrogen. The *Hindenburg* held seven million cubic feet of hydrogen gas.

Since the early 1920s, American airships had used helium, a nonflammable gas. Helium was more expensive than hydrogen and hard to obtain. The United States was the only nation with large supplies of it. The U.S. government would not sell helium to Germany because they did not trust Hitler. They feared he might use zeppelins to carry weapons and attack other nations. This was a very tense time in history. By late 1939, Hitler's Nazi soldiers would invade Poland and set off World War II.

The hydrogen used in German airships was lighter

The *Hindenburg* flies above Olympic Stadium in Germany while opening ceremonies of the 1936 Olympics are held on August 1, 1936.

than helium. Hydrogen is a flammable gas, however. It will burn if it catches fire. Because of this, zeppelins were carefully designed to prevent fires. The gas cells were tightly sealed. Each cell had its own controls. Miles of metal wires and netting held the cells in place.

Nothing that could create even a spark was allowed on a zeppelin. The crew wore special shoes with felt soles. These shoes did not create static electricity on the floors. Only special sealed flashlights could be used on board, and no flashbulbs were allowed. Fire extinguishers were located throughout the ship. A crew member called a rigger checked the gas cells carefully for holes or leaks.

*T*his advertising brochure sketch shows the control and navigation car of the *Hindenburg*.

Electricians were also part of the crew. If a wire failed, they could fix it at once.

The crew let out gas to lower the zeppelin. This made the zeppelin act heavier. The gas left the airship through special chimneys. It blew behind the airship as it flew along. Drums inside the zeppelin were filled with water. The crew would let out some of this water to lighten the load of the airship. This allowed the ship to rise more quickly. The ship would also dump water before landing so ground crews could more easily direct it.

Four rudders attached to the tail fins helped to steer the *Hindenburg*. A backup control section was built inside the lower fin. The captain could use it if the main controls failed. There were twelve mechanics. One mechanic was always on duty in each of the four engine gondolas. A gondola is a long, narrow compartment attached underneath an airship.

The Zeppelin Company urged travelers to choose the *Hindenburg*. One advertising booklet was called "Across the Ocean by Airship!" It said that "a voyage across the ocean above the clouds can be added to others in this age of wonders."[3] The booklet said passengers would be "dazzled by [the *Hindenburg's*] immense size and the beauty of its silver grey form."[4] It promised a pleasant takeoff: "There is no delay, you have felt no shock, no tremble or vibration, and yet you notice the ship is moving."[5] According to these ads, "People are never sick on board an airship. . . . The air is delicious and fresh."[6]

Hundreds of passengers agreed. The *Hindenburg*

crossed the Atlantic Ocean twenty-one times in 1936. People eagerly awaited the 1937 season. The first flight that year took place in March. It went from Germany to South America. Then the *Hindenburg* was grounded for a month while nine new cabins were added to her lower deck. This boosted the airship's capacity from fifty to seventy-two passengers. Soon the enlarged ship would head for the United States.

The *Hindenburg* is shown here dumping water in order to ensure a smooth landing.

A "Flying Hotel"

Excited passengers prepared to depart on May 3. Soon they would board the famous *Hindenburg*. They had paid a high price for their tickets. A flight from Germany to America cost $400—the price of a small car. Round-trip tickets were $720.

The zeppelin looked even larger in person. Its silver shell rippled in the wind. Some passengers said the fabric looked thin. However, the crew assured them it was very strong.

Thirty-six men, women, and children climbed aboard for this trip. Some of them had already flown in a zeppelin. They told the others it was a great way to travel. Passenger Edith Dieckmann later said, "We were completely overwhelmed by the ship. We were very conscious that this was a unique and magnificent experience that might never come again."[1]

A few of the passengers were well known. Joseph Spah was a famous stage actor and acrobat. Spah was originally born in Germany, but later immigrated to the United States when the Nazis rose to power. Spah had brought a prize dog named Ulla along. He planned to give it to his children in America. Animals traveled in the storage area.

In addition to the other passengers, there were sixty-one crew members on board. Captain Ernst Lehmann and Captain Max Pruss were in charge. They were two of the company's top pilots. Emmi Imhof was the stewardess. Imhof was the first airship stewardess in history. Her job

*T*his is a sketch of a typical passenger's cabin aboard the *Hindenburg*.

was to help make passengers comfortable. She answered questions and helped people find their way around.

Security men were also on board. They were members of the German military. Their job was to prevent sabotage on the airship. Hitler had enemies around the world. In 1935, a time bomb had been found on the *Graf Zeppelin.*

A brass band played German patriotic songs as passengers came on board. Officials had already checked everyone's baggage carefully. Now they asked passengers to turn over any matches, cigarette lighters, or flashbulbs. There were other important rules. Passengers were forbidden to throw anything overboard. Flying objects might hurt the propellers or hull. They were not allowed to leave the passenger area without a crew member.

Captain Lehmann stood in the control car. "Schiff hoch!—Up ship!" he ordered.[2] Soon the *Hindenburg* rose smoothly up into the air. When it was high enough, the four engines were turned on. Yet there was hardly any noise. Passenger Louis Lochner wrote in his diary: "You feel as though you were carried in the arms of angels."[3]

Some passengers asked to tour the ship. They admired the tidy cabins. There were showers and washrooms with hot and cold water. The dining room was on the port side. White linens covered the tables. Fine china and fresh flowers were in place. One big attraction was the piano in the lounge. It was made of aluminum covered with tan pigskin. The piano weighed just 397 pounds.

Passengers were amazed by the walkway inside the airship. It ran along the whole length of the *Hindenburg.*

*L*anding lines attached to the gondola of the *Hindenburg* anchor the airship to the ground at the U.S. Naval Station in Lakehurst, N.J., on May 11, 1935.

The crew used it to get around. Quarters for the crew and passengers took about one-fifth of the space inside one gas cell. The crew slept inside small tents with canvas flaps.

That first night out, the *Hindenburg* passed over Germany. It soared above the countryside of Holland. May 4 was a Tuesday. The airship moved smoothly through cloudy skies.

By Wednesday, passengers had settled into a routine. They read, played bridge or other card games, chatted, or wrote letters. Some spent hours looking out of the observation windows. At night, some men gathered in the downstairs smoking room and bar. This room was tightly sealed and lined with asbestos, a fireproof material. A single electric lighter was attached to a wall in the room. This was the only place on board where passengers could smoke.

Passengers looked forward to mealtimes. The *Hindenburg's* storeroom was well stocked. It held eight hundred eggs and more than four hundred pounds of

*A*bove is a sketch of the *Hindenburg's* smoking room.

26

poultry and other meats. There were stacks of cheeses and hundreds of bottles of fine wine. One dinner included soup, roast duck, filet of sole, vegetables, and cheeses and pastries. Fresh rolls and breads were baked and served each day.

As the *Hindenburg* made its way to the North American coast, there were fascinating things to see. Large and small icebergs floated on the ocean. Passengers spotted a few large blue whales. They leaped above the ocean's surface and sprayed water from their spouts. Seagulls fluttered in the air.

The *Hindenburg* was supposed to land at an air station in Lakehurst, New Jersey. The air station was run by the U.S. Navy, which had been developing airships to act as scouts for its fleets. (At the time, the U.S. Air Force did not yet exist as a separate military branch.) In addition to the *Hindenburg*, the Lakehurst station had previously housed many other famous ships. Among them were the U.S.S. *Los Angeles*, the U.S.S. *Akron*, and the *Shenandoah*. The round-the-world flight of the *Graf Zeppelin* also began and ended at Lakehurst.

The *Hindenburg* was due to land at Lakehurst on the morning of May 6, but stormy weather put it behind schedule. Passenger Leonhard Adelt later wrote that the airship was "a gray object in a gray mist, over the invisible sea."[4] Passengers tried to see Boston through the mist. Outside Boston, passenger Margaret Mather saw homes and gardens. She later said, "Yellow forsythia was in bloom, and some sort of trailing pink; the grass plots were vivid green." Mather also saw "apple trees in blossom and woods full of dogwood and young green leaves."[5]

The clouds parted as the zeppelin crossed New York City. Passengers glimpsed tall buildings and the Statue of Liberty. Leonhard Adelt said the skyscrapers looked "like

*T*he *Hindenburg* is shown here moored in a hangar at the Naval air station in Lakehurst on May 9, 1936, just a year before its final, fatal trip.

a board full of nails."[6] New Yorkers waved from the streets. Some drivers honked their horns.

Rain began to fall as the *Hindenburg* headed southeast for New Jersey. As the ship neared the Lakehurst air station, the captains found they could not land because of the weather. So instead, they took the *Hindenburg* down the coast. Captain Pruss sent a message to the naval control station at Lakehurst. It said, "We will wait your report that landing conditions are better."[7] The crew served the passengers sandwiches on silver trays.

Finally the captains were told to go back to Lakehurst. The weather was still cloudy. Lightning could be seen in the sky. The naval station sent a message saying, "Conditions now suitable for landing ground crew is ready."[8] They arrived about twelve hours late.

The crew were ordered to their stations. At last the *Hindenburg* would land.

A Ball of Fire

Hundreds of spectators waited on the airfield below the *Hindenburg*. Verna Thomas was among them. She recalled the weather that day. "It was raining very badly, an electrical storm," Thomas said.[1]

Some spectators waved. Flashbulbs popped as they photographed the famous airship and its smiling passengers. Newsreel photographers aimed their movie cameras at the *Hindenburg*. Reporters wrote in their notebooks. Radio announcer Herbert Morrison called the airship "a great floating palace."[2] He told his listeners, "The sun is striking the windows . . . and sparkling like glittering jewels against a background of black velvet."[3] Morrison continued his report: "It's coming down out of the sky pointed directly toward us."[4]

The *Hindenburg* was about two hundred feet above the ground. Suddenly the ship began to shake. Passengers heard a loud noise. People on the ground gasped. They stared at the airship in horror. Flames were shooting from

S pectators watched in awe as the *Hindenburg* flew high in the sky above them, just hours before the ship would burst into flames and crash.

the *Hindenburg*. Pieces of the ship fell to the ground in flames. Spectators ran away, screaming.

Passengers later recalled feeling a jolt. Crew member Eugen Bentele said, "My first thought was that the landing crew had pulled too hard and something had broken. But that wasn't it. When I looked out, I saw flames shooting forward from the rear of the *Hindenburg* toward my engine car."[5] Then Bentele passed out for a few seconds.

On the ground, Herbert Morrison was still broadcasting over the radio. Now he sounded greatly distressed.

He said, "It's burst into flames. . . . Get out of the way, please, oh my, this is terrible, oh my, get out of the way, please! It is burning, bursting into flames and is falling. . . . Oh! This is one of the worst catastrophes in the world! . . . Oh, the humanity and all the passengers!"[6] Then Morrison said, "I can't talk, ladies and gentlemen, I'm sorry. I must step inside where I can't see it."[7]

Inside the airship, people saw a bright flash of light. They lost their balance as the floor slanted. Furniture and other objects bounced around. Flames shot through the plane. They burned up the carpeting and everything else they touched. Smoke poured through the rooms. Passengers could barely see as they tried to escape the intense heat that surrounded them.

Some crew in the extra control station escaped. They dashed out as the lower tail fin touched ground. Other people jumped as they came closer to the ground. They landed amid flaming wreckage. People covered with soot and burns ran or crawled away from the fire. Some people's clothing had burned off.

John Iannaccone was part of the Navy ground crew. He watched a man trying to escape. Iannaccone said, "He walked out of the ship after the nose of the ship was on the ground. He didn't have a stitch of clothes on. And everything was burned . . . the only thing he had on him was his shoes."[8] This man died soon afterward.

Alfred Grozinger was a cook on the *Hindenburg*. He recalled, "I thought my end had come. But suddenly there was the ground. Luckily it was sandy and soft and I had

The *Hindenburg* crashes to the ground tail-first after exploding in a giant ball of fire on May 6, 1937.

more or less fallen on my feet. Immediately I picked myself up and ran away."[9]

People watched the scene in horror. Verna Thomas recalled hearing other spectators say, "Oh, God, oh God." She said, "There was nothing you could do. All I could do was just look . . . and cry."[10]

Captain Ernst Lehmann staggered out of the burning ship. He was badly burned. Someone heard him say, "I couldn't understand it."[11]

American naval officers tried to help people coming out of the airship. Sirens screamed as ambulances sped to the scene. They carried the injured and the dead into

*T*he shell of the *Hindenburg* continues to burn after crashing to the ground. American naval officers rush toward the ship to help its passengers.

the zeppelin's empty hangar. Some victims cried in pain. Others were too stunned to speak.

People who heard the radio broadcast were shocked and horrified. Newspapers carried the story. A headline in *The New York Times* compared the *Hindenburg* to "a giant torch."[12]

The airship burned up within minutes. The ground fires went on for hours. When it ended, the remains of the airship lay on the ground. Bits of blackened cloth were all that remained of the silver covering. Smoke blew around the crumpled metal frame. Metal objects, including some coins and eating utensils, were scattered on the ground. A horrible smell filled the air.

People felt sad and confused. What could have gone wrong? Mechanic John Iannaccone would later say, "You couldn't fathom how something like that could happen."[13]

What Went Wrong?

The next day, guards stood by the site of the wreckage. Nobody was allowed to touch anything until experts could inspect it. They had to rope off the area. Souvenir hunters had been picking up items from the ground.

The Zeppelin Company was shocked by the terrible news. Hugo Eckener said, "That can't be!"[1] The company canceled its other trans-Atlantic flights.

Newspapers reported that thirteen passengers had died. Twenty-two crew members on board and one crew member on the ground also lost their lives. Captain Lehmann and stewardess Emmi Imhof both died. Captain Pruss was badly burned while trying to rescue others. In some families, some members survived while others did not. Teenage Irene Doehner and her father died. Irene's mother and her two brothers were safe.

Rumors spread about the cause of the fire. Was it sabotage? Did someone hide an explosive device on board? No evidence of a bomb was found. Maybe someone from

*T*his aerial photo of the wreckage of the *Hindenburg* was taken on May 7, 1937, the day after the explosion.

the ground had shot at the airship? A game hunter, perhaps?

Both the Americans and Germans wanted to know what had happened. German government investigators arrived in Lakehurst. Officials from the Zeppelin Company also came to America. They studied the remains of the airship.

The sixty-two survivors told their stories. They described what happened before, during, and after the fire. Investigators also talked with people who were on the ground that day.

The Federal Bureau of Investigation checked the backgrounds of the passengers and crew. Some people suspected the acrobat Joseph Spah. He was known to oppose the Nazi government. Also, he was a skilled acrobat and had leaped safely from the burning ship. But no evidence against him was found.

Investigators then considered mechanical failure. They looked for problems in the airship's design. People began blaming the hydrogen gas. There was no clear evidence that gas had leaked from a cell. Still, investigators said a leak must have occurred. Perhaps, they speculated, a buildup of static electricity on the shell of the ship caused a spark. A spark mixed with leaking gas

*I*nvestigators sift through the wreckage of the *Hindenburg*, searching for clues that might reveal how the fire started.

could have started the fire. The U.S. Department of Commerce issued a sixty-three-page report. One section said, "The cause of the accident was the ignition of a mixture of free hydrogen and air."[2] Many people accepted this theory.

The Zeppelin Company stopped making commercial flights. In 1939, the first passenger airplane flights began. The Germans took apart their remaining airships during World War II (1939–1945). They used the metal for other military products.

Some people continued to wonder about the *Hindenburg* fire. New theories were suggested during the 1990s. Addison Bain is a retired engineer from NASA (National Aeronautics and Space Administration). He is a hydrogen expert. Bain disagreed with the gas leak theory. He said, "There was no physical evidence building to the conclusion. . . there was no testing done."[3]

Bain spent nine years looking into the cause of the fire. He studied bits of the *Hindenburg* wreckage and conducted scientific tests. Bain also made models of the airship, using the same materials. He talked with survivors and studied films of the disaster.

In 1997, Bain reported his findings at a meeting of the National Hydrogen Association. He said hydrogen did not cause the blaze. Bain explained that the zeppelin did not explode. It burned along certain patterns. He found that the fire had begun around the fin on the starboard side of the airship. Witness Helmut Lau had said, "The first burning out of the fire was on the starboard side,

*E*lisabeth Veil, granddaughter of Ferdinand von Zeppelin, stands before the *Friedrichshafen* on July 2, 2000. New zeppelins like the *Friedrichshafen* are much smaller than the *Hindenburg* and are designed to take much shorter journeys.

above and up."[4] A hydrogen fire could have come only from a vent on the airship.

The pieces of fabric that fell off the zeppelin were aflame. These flames were bright red and orange. Hydrogen flames are blue and burn upward.

What caused the fire, then? Bain suspected a problem in the fabric used for the shell. Airship historian Hepburn Walker had saved bits of the *Hindenburg*'s shell. Bain studied them to find out what chemicals were used to coat the fabric. A liquid called dope protected the cloth shell. It made the shell waterproof.

A new dope formula had been used on the

Hindenburg. Bain found that it had an oil base and contained iron oxide and aluminum dust. These same ingredients are now used to make rocket fuel. Bain tested fabric coated with these ingredients. When it was ignited, it burned within seconds.

Bain's theory stated that static electrical charges probably built up on the shell through normal flying. This could have caused a spark. The airship had also spent hours in an electrical storm. Lightning may have struck the *Hindenburg*. One witness saw a blue glow at the top of the zeppelin just before the fire.

Letters found in Germany support this theory. A German engineer wrote one of these letters in June 1937. It said, "The actual cause of the fire was the extreme easy

*T*oday, companies like Goodyear use blimps for advertising purposes. Goodyear blimps can often be seen flying above sporting events.

flammability of the covering material brought about by discharges of an electrostatic nature."[5] Bain found out that German scientists had done secret tests in 1937, after the crash. They learned that the coating on the *Hindenburg* may have caused the fire. But the government covered up these findings. The Zeppelin Company did make some changes as a result of these tests, however, using graphite lacing cords on the next ship, the *LZ130*.

Today passenger jets carry people across the seas. Zeppelins are not used for commercial travel. Just a few dozen airships operate. These ships, called blimps, are quiet and safe. They are buoyed by helium and are used mostly for advertising. Sea World, Metropolitan Life Insurance, and Fuji are three companies that own blimps. Some blimps contain TV cameras. They float above sports events with their cameras running.

Scientists also use blimps. They scan the ocean taking pictures of whales, dolphins, or other marine life. Blimps make it possible for them to "park" in the air and observe the animals without bothering them.

The *Hindenburg* disaster has not been forgotten. A *Hindenburg* memorial was built in Lakehurst, New Jersey. Every year, the Navy Lakehurst Historical Society holds a memorial service on May 6. At 7:25 P.M. it honors those who have died in all airship accidents through the years. Like the name *Titanic*, the name *Hindenburg* now stands for tragedy.

Other Airship Disasters

DATE	PLACE	DISASTER
June 14, 1887	Germany	Karl Wolfert and his mechanic, Hans Knabe, become the first men to die in an airship when the ship's carburetor sets off the hydrogen-filled envelope.
August 24, 1921	Kingston-on-Hull, England	The *R38* crashes due to structural failure. Forty-four die; five survive.
February 21, 1922	Langley Field, Virginia	The *Roma*, a semirigid dirigible, crashes due to a possible elevator problem. Thirty-four die; eleven survive.
December 21, 1923	Pantallaria, south of Sicily	The *Dixmude* goes down. Fifty-two fatalities; no survivors.
September 3, 1925	Ava, Ohio	The helium-buoyed *Shenandoah* crashes as a result of bad weather conditions. Fourteen die; twenty-eight survive.
May 24, 1928	The North Pole	Climatic conditions cause the *Italia*, a semirigid dirigible, to crash. Seven die; nine survive.
October 4, 1930	Beauvais, France	The *R101* goes down as a result of pilot error. Forty-eight people die; six survive.
April 14, 1933	Barnegat, New Jersey	The helium ship the *Akron* crashes due to poor weather. Seventy-three die; only three survive.

Chapter Notes

Chapter 1. Thirty-Four Seconds of Terror

1. Rick Archbold, *Hindenburg: Reliving the Era of the Great Airships* (Toronto: Madison Press Books, 1994), p. 180.

2. Michael Macdonald Mooney, *The Hindenburg* (New York: Dodd, Mead & Co., 1972), p. 234.

3. "What Happened to the *Hindenburg*," *Secrets of the Dead*, prod. Beth C. Hoppe and Dan Chambers, PBS documentary series, broadcast May 17, 2000.

4. Craig Thompson, "Airship Like a Giant Torch on Darkening Jersey Field," *The New York Times*, May 7, 1937, p. A-1.

5. Archbold, p. 187.

Chapter 2. Lighter Than Air

1. Rick Archbold, *Hindenburg: Reliving the Era of the Great Airships* (Toronto: Madison Press Books, 1994), p. 10.

2. Archbold, p. 21.

3. "Across the Ocean by AIRSHIP!," *The Zeppelin Ring*, n.d., <http://www.airships.net/book3.jpg> (April 28, 2000).

4. "The Voyage Begins," *The Zeppelin Ring*, n.d., <http://www.airships.net/book9.jpg> (April 28, 2000).

5. Ibid.

6. "A Day On Board," *The Zeppelin Ring*, n.d., <http://www.airships.net/book13.jpg> (April 28, 2000).

Chapter 3. A "Flying Hotel"

1. "What Happened to the *Hindenburg*," *Secrets of the Dead*, prod. Beth C. Hoppe and Dan Chambers, PBS documentary series, broadcast May 17, 2000.

2. Rick Archbold, *Hindenburg: Reliving the Era of the Great Airships* (Toronto: Madison Press Books, 1994), p. 161.

3. Ibid., p. 162.

4. Ibid., p. 174.

5. Michael Macdonald Mooney, *The Hindenburg* (New York: Dodd, Mead & Co., 1972), p. 222.

6. Ibid., p. 223.

7. Ibid., p. 226.

8. Ibid., p. 228.

Chapter 4. A Ball of Fire

1. "What Happened to the *Hindenburg*," *Secrets of the Dead*, prod. Beth C. Hoppe and Dan Chambers, PBS documentary series, broadcast May 17, 2000.

2. Michael Macdonald Mooney, *The Hindenburg* (New York: Dodd, Mead & Co., 1972), p. 234.

3. Rick Archbold, *Hindenburg: Reliving the Era of the Great Airships* (Toronto: Madison Press Books, 1994), p. 180.

4. Ibid.

5. "What Happened to the Hindenburg."

6. Archbold, p. 183.

7. Russell Foster, "Ship Falls Ablaze," *The New York Times*, May 7, 1937, p. A-1.

8. "What Happened to the Hindenburg."

9. Ibid.

10. Ibid.

11. Foster, p. A-1.

12. Craig Thompson, "Airship Like a Giant Torch on Darkening Jersey Field," *The New York Times*, May 7, 1937, p. A-1.

13. Associated Press, "Controversy Over the Hindenburg Disaster Still Burns," n.d., <http://www.ttcorp.com/nha/pr_ap97a.htm> (June 10, 2000).

Chapter 5. What Went Wrong?

1. Rick Archbold, *Hindenburg: Reliving the Era of the Great Airships* (Toronto: Madison Press Books, 1994), p. 196.

2. "The Hindenburg Accident," report from Department of Commerce Bureau of Air Commerce, Safety and Planning Commission, June 1937.

3. "What Happened to the *Hindenburg*," *Secrets of the Dead*, prod. Beth C. Hoppe and Dan Chambers, PBS documentary series, broadcast May 17, 2000.

4. Ibid.

5. Jacquelyn Cochran Bokow, "Hydrogen Exonerated in Hindenburg Disaster," *NHA News*, volume 2, no. 2, Spring 1997, <http://www.ttcorp.com/nha/advocate/ad22zepp.htm> (April 19, 2000).

airship—A vessel that moves through the air.

asbestos—A fireproof material.

balloonist—A person who rides in a balloon.

cabin—A private room on a ship.

cell—A receptacle or bag that contains the gas aboard an airship.

dirigible—A craft that moves or floats through the air.

dope—Absorbent material used in different manufacturing operations.

fin—An airfoil attached to an airship to keep it directionally stable.

gondola—A long, narrow compartment attached underneath an airship.

helium—A nonflammable gas that is lighter than air.

hydrogen—A highly flammable gas that is lighter than air.

rigger—Someone who fits a ship with rigging.

rudder—A movable airfoil that helps steer an airship.

zeppelin—A rigid airship with a cylinder-shaped frame.

Althoff, William F. *Sky Ships: A History of the Airship in the United States Navy.* Pacifica, Calif.: Pacifica Military History, 1998.

Armentrout, Patricia. *Extreme Machines in the Air.* Vero Beach, Fla.: Rourke Press, Inc., 1998.

Donkin, Andrew. *Zeppelin: The Age of the Airship.* New York: Dorling Kindersley Publishing, Inc., 1999.

Hedin, Robert, ed. *The Zeppelin Reader: Stories, Poems, & Songs from the Age of Airships.* Iowa City: University of Iowa Press, 1998.

Icanberry, Mark. *Picnic on a Cloud.* Kensington, Calif.: Look, Learn & Do Publications, 1999.

Majoor, Mireille. *Inside the Hindenburg.* New York: Little, Brown & Co., 2000.

O'Brien, Patrick. *The Hindenburg.* New York: Henry Holt Co., 2000.

Recks, Robert J. *Building Gas Blimps.* Grass Valley, Calif.: Recks Publications, 1997.

Stille, Darlene R. *Blimps.* Danbury, Conn.: Children's Press, 1997.

Tanaka, Shelley. *The Disaster of the Hindenburg: The Last Flight of the Greatest Airship Ever Built.* New York: Scholastic, Inc., 1996.

The Hindenburg Historical Society
http://www.hindenburg.net/

Navy Lakehurst Historical Society
http://www.nlhs.com/

The Hindenburg Disaster
http://www.vidicom-tv.com/tohiburg.html

Airships: The Zeppelin History and Photo Website
http://www.airships.net/